Myra Brooks-Turner Piano Duo Collection

Mill Stream Medley

(2 Pianos - 4 Hands)

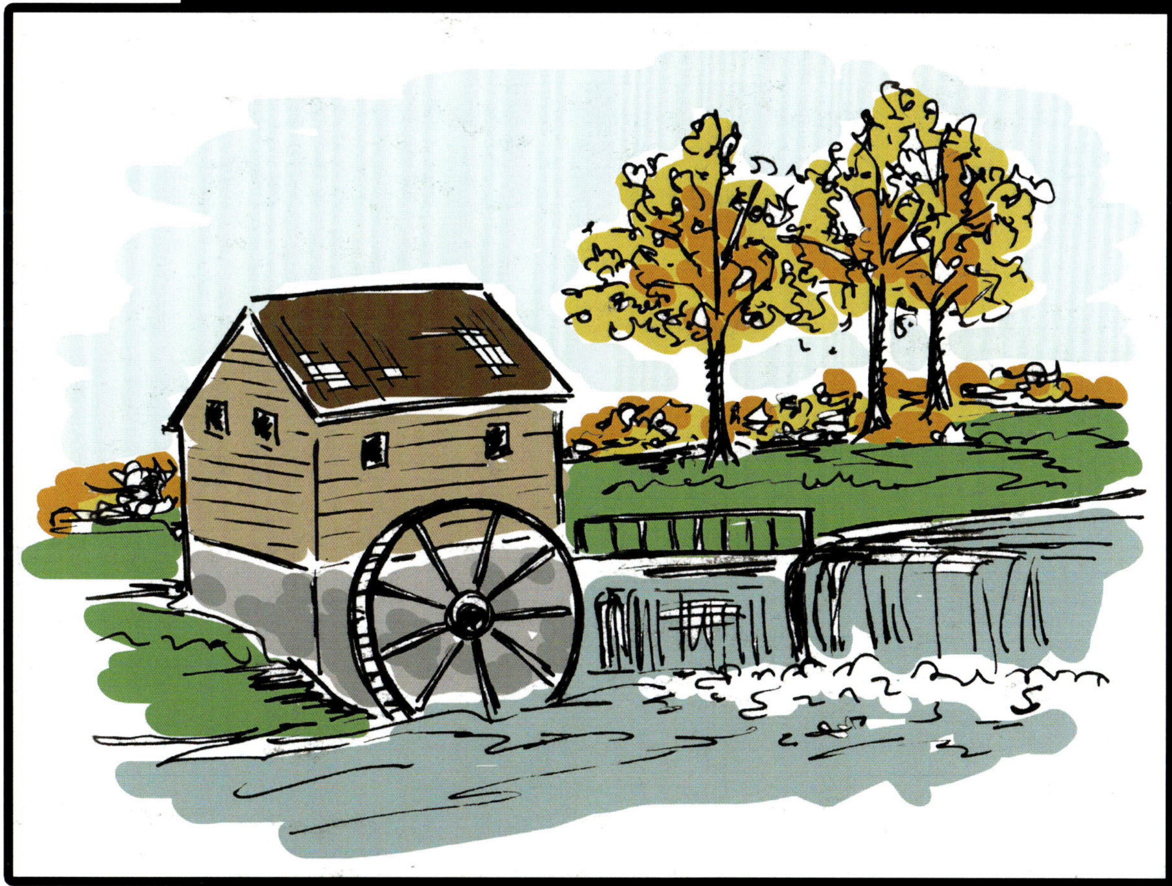

Mill Stream Medley

To Charlotte and Ed Walden

Tell Taylor
Arr. by Myra Brooks-Turner, Op. 75 No. 3

Schaum Publications, Inc.
10235 N. Port Washington Rd.
Mequon, WI 53092
www.schaumpiano.net

Level Six

ISBN 978-1-62906-013-2

EXCLUSIVELY DISTRIBUTED BY
HAL LEONARD

00645841
U.S. $3.99   7111